Mi taku ogasin—"We are all related."

Lakota chant

KACHINA DOLLS
Hopi. Late nineteenth/early twentieth century. Painted wood, cloth, feathers, string, and yarn (sinew used in doll at left).
Left, 16" h.; *right*, approximately 15" h.

COME
LOOK WITH ME

Exploring Native American Art With Children

Stephanie Salomon

LICKLE PUBLISHING INC

First published in 1997 by Lickle Publishing Inc
590 Madison Avenue, New York, NY 10022

Library of Congress Cataloging-in-Publication Data
Salomon, Stephanie.
    Come look with me : exploring Native American art with
children / Stephanie Salomon
        p.   cm.
    ISBN (invalid) 096503081
    1. Indian art—North American—Juvenile literature. I. Title.
CORR E98.A7S25   1997
704.03'97—dc21   97-31465
                                                        CIP
                                                        AC

Director, Editorial, Production & Design: Charles Davey
COME LOOK WITH ME Series Editor: Stephanie Salomon
Production Editor: Stacey Guttman
Senior Designer: Betty Lew

Printed in Hong Kong

For Claire

This book is dedicated to Gladys S. Blizzard,
who conceived the idea for and the title
Come Look With Me. Her goal was to stimulate children
to look at art with enjoyment and to teach adults and
children to take pleasure in looking at art together.
Unfortunately, Gladys Blizzard died after the first four
books in the series were published. It is hoped that the
continuation of the series honors her memory.

Acknowledgments
Many sources have been consulted in the making of this publication, in
particular, the following books and exhibition catalogues on Native
American arts: Anne D'Aleva, *Native American Arts and Cultures*
(Worcester, Mass.: Davis Publications, Inc.,1993); Tom Hill and Richard
W. Hill, Sr., eds., *Creation's Journey: Native American Identity and Belief*
(Washington, D.C.: Smithsonian Institution Press, in association with
the National Museum of the American Indian, 1994); Gilbert T. Vincent,
Masterpieces of American Indian Art from the Eugene and Clare Thaw Collection
(New York: Harry N. Abrams, Inc., Publishers, in association with The
New York State Historical Association, 1995); and Janet Catherine
Berlo, ed., *Plains Indian Drawings 1865–1935: Pages from a Visual History*
(New York: Harry N. Abrams, Inc., Publishers, in association with The
American Federation of Arts and The Drawing Center, 1996). The
institutions that provided the photographs reproduced on these pages
are also gratefully acknowledged: the Museum of the American Indian,
Fenimore House Museum of The New York State Historical Association,
and the American Museum of Natural History. These works are
individually credited on page 32.

Contents

Preface

Traditional art forms created by Native Americans (also known as "American Indians") are among the oldest in North America. They can be considered the "first" American art. Many, like rock art and stone and wood carving existed long before the arrival of Europeans on the continent. Others, like painting and drawing on paper, or beadwork, mixed Native elements with European media. This book presents a selection of different kinds of traditional Native American art, focusing on North America and made up of examples that speak to children. It is not meant to be comprehensive, or representative of the vast and rich diversity of work created by the many peoples that we group together as Native American.

It is often said that to look at and learn about Native American arts, we must see not only with our eyes but also with our hearts. Native American languages do not have a word for "art" as something separated from other parts of life. For non-Natives, art generally means paintings, drawings, and sculpture. In traditional Native cultures, works of art had a purpose—a drum used in a ceremony, a mask or shirt made for a special feast, a toy figure carved for teaching grown-up ways to children. Beautifully designed and constructed objects were part of the beauty of everyday living.

How to use this book

COME LOOK WITH ME: *Exploring Native American Art with Children* is the sixth in the *Come Look with Me* series of art appreciation books for young people. Like the previous books, it is intended to be shared with one child or with a small group of children.

A sequence of questions designed to provide a basis for discussion and thought accompanies each of the twelve works selected. Since the individual creators of many examples of traditional Native American art are unknown, and because the role of a given object within its culture is so important, the background texts that appear on each page are also meant to be considered in conjunction with the questions. These texts can be read silently or aloud, or paraphrased for children while the book is open to the picture.

Encourage each child to point to parts of the object or picture while he or she talks about it. If you are sharing this book with a group, always ask if anyone has a different idea. That different idea might spark further thinking and conversation, and every answer is valuable. Our various experiences, traditions, ages, and points of view can bring great benefits to a group discussion. Interaction will be kept lively if a session focuses on just two or three selections at a time.

The works pictured in *Come Look with Me*, or ones similar to them, may increasingly be found in museums and Native American cultural centers that are dedicated to presenting the history and art of Native peoples. Festivals or events open to the public also provide a look at how ceremonial wear and other objects were used. Demonstrations of traditional artistic techniques are offered in many of these settings. While there is no substitute for seeing the colors, textures, materials, and size of original works, this book can help both children and adults to approach traditional Native American art with greater understanding and delight and to share their insights and enthusiasms with others.

HORSE MASK
Nez Perce. ca. 1875–1900. Woolen cloth, cotton, glass beads, brass buttons, dyed horsehair, silk ribbons, feathers, brass-framed mirror, hide, cotton thread, and ermine. 40" h. × 32" w.

What clues tell you that this is a mask for a horse?

The horse mask was used to "dress" a horse on important occasions. Does this mask seem out of the ordinary to you? Why or why not?

When the Nez Perce people traded their horses for beaded objects, they learned something about the art and designs of other Native tribes, in particular, the Crow Indians. Compare the beadwork on this horse mask with the designs on the Crow boy's shirt on page 20. In what ways are they the same? In what ways are they different?

Why do you think there is a small mirror attached to the mask?

Breeding horses and riding them were specialties of the Nez Perce (pronounced "Nezz Purse") Indians. The name by which we now know this group comes from the French words for "pierced nose." In the early 1800s French explorers came upon members of the tribe who wore nose ornaments made from shells. The areas that today make up eastern Oregon and Washington, Idaho, and Montana, where the Nez Perce lived before the twentieth century, were ideal places for keeping horses, and the animals thrived in the grass-covered river valleys. Families kept herds of horses—some herds numbered a few hundred animals.

Nez Perce horses were famous for their great size and strength. One favorite was the spotted Appaloosa. Neighboring Native groups were eager to trade beadwork and other goods for them. The Nez Perce gave much attention to their horses and outfitted them with beautifully decorated harnesses, blankets, and other gear. This showed their respect for the animal.

Originally used during battle preparations, horse masks later became part of the tribe's twentieth-century celebrations. Of all the Native groups, the Nez Perce used the brightest colors in their decorations—like the strong reds and blues in the mask pictured here. The mask also features horsehair dyed in several colors and a small, shiny real mirror in a frame.

KACHINA DOLLS
Hopi. Late nineteenth/early twentieth century. Painted wood, cloth, feathers, string, and yarn (sinew used in doll at left).
Left, 16" h.; *right*, approximately 15" h.

10

＋

Have you ever received a doll or figure as a gift? Who gave it to you? Talk about a toy or something you own that is very special to you.

How old do you think a child playing with these dolls would be? Why do you think so?

What do you think these dolls are made of? Name and point to the different kinds of materials that you see used.

Kachinas, or powerful spirits, are important in Hopi life and celebrations. The Hopi, one of the Pueblo Indian peoples, live in the American Southwest, which includes states like New Mexico and Arizona. The name Hopi means "peaceful"—living peacefully among animals, plants, and other human beings. It also means "good" and "wise."

There are more than 300 different Kachinas. Each one stands for a different animal (like the buffalo), plant (like corn), part of nature (like the sun or the rain), or human quality (like bravery). During thrilling ceremonies, adult male Hopis paint their bodies and wear costumes, jewelry, headdresses, and sometimes, masks to represent the different Kachinas. They perform dances that "talk" to the spirits, asking them to bring rain (the Southwest is hot and dry), make crops grow, or drive away sickness. Children learn about the Kachinas by watching the dances.

Kachina dolls like the ones here had a special place in the lives of the Hopi children who lived almost one hundred years ago. They were carved by adults (mostly men) out of cottonwood and then painted and dressed to look like the dancers. The Kachina dancers would give the dolls to Hopi children, generally girls, during the celebrations as blessings for a happy life. The first doll received by a child as an infant would be flat and very simple. As children grew older, the dolls had more details and decorations.

The doll on the right represents Aholi who accompanies Eototo, the "father of the Kachinas," during the Powamu ceremony (Bean Dance) held in February. Aholi can be recognized by his pointed helmet and staff. With the staff, mythical Aholi traces symbols of clouds that Eototo has formed on the ground out of cornmeal so that rainclouds will come to the Hopi villages. The doll on the left stands for Nakiachop, the Silent Warrior, who is very daring and brave.

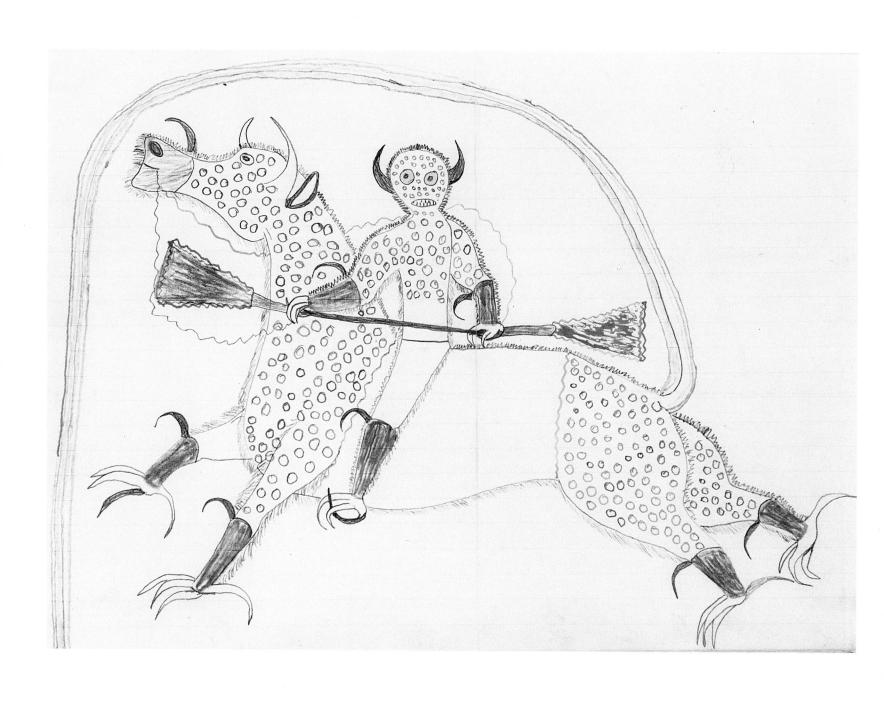

"DREAM OR VISION OF HIMSELF CHANGED TO A DESTROYER OR RIDING A BUFFALO EAGLE"
From *Drawing Book* by Black Hawk (Sans Arc Lakota). 1880–81. Pencil, colored pencil, and ink on paper.
10¼" l. × 16½" w.

Have you ever seen creatures that look like these? Do they look like animals? People? Do they look real or imaginary? Explain.

Do the animal and its rider look friendly or frightening? Why do you think so? Choose three words to describe the creatures.

Find and trace a wavy line with your finger. Find the beginning of the horse's tail. Find its end.

Have you ever imagined you were someone else—an animal? How would you look? Draw a picture of what you would look like.

Black Hawk, the artist who made this drawing, was said to be a medicine man—someone with special powers who could cure sickness. He was a member of the Lakota Sioux, one of the Plains Indian tribes. The Lakota lived in the buffalo territory of what is now South Dakota, Montana, Wyoming, and Nebraska.

This picture comes from a book of seventy-five drawings. They are known as "ledger book" drawings because they were made in an account book, or ledger. European-American traders used ledgers to keep track of their business. If you look closely, you can see that the paper is lined for this purpose; it might also remind you of paper used in a classroom.

Black Hawk used colored pencil and ink on paper to show scenes from nature, hunting, Lakota dances and ceremonies, and dreams or visions. Plains Indians traditionally painted the same kinds of pictures on buffalo hides, especially those used for the walls of tipis.

In this drawing Black Hawk tried to show something dream-like. A mighty Thunder Being, a spirit-creature who lives in the sky, is pictured as part horse, part buffalo, and part eagle, with a tail that turns into a rainbow. Icy hail, drawn as spots, fall on the mythical creature and its rider as they fly through the air. The artist imagined himself as the rider, with horns and claws and bright yellow eyes. The wavy lines that surround him stand for strength and power.

SHAWNEE CHICKEN DANCE
Ernest Spybuck (Absentee Shawnee). ca. 1910. Watercolor, graphite, and crayon on paperboard.
24½" l. × 17½" w.

Objects or people that we see in the distance look smaller than ones that are near. Spybuck was one of the first Native painters to use perspective—showing objects close to us and far away as they appear to our eyes. What do you see in the front of the picture? The middle? The back?

Can you find any animals?

What kinds of things in the picture tell us that the people are dancing? Do they look as if they are celebrating? Why or why not?

If you were to paint a celebration you know, what would it be?

When he was quite young, Ernest Spybuck, a member of the Shawnee tribe, taught himself to draw and paint with watercolors. Spybuck was born on a reservation—land set aside for Native peoples—in Oklahoma in 1883, so he never knew what it was like to travel, farm, and hunt freely in the homeland of his parents and grandparents. That land was the Ohio River Valley, which includes parts of present-day Indiana, Pennsylvania, and Kentucky. Spybuck attended the Shawnee Boarding School (in earlier times, Native children did not learn at schools but from other members of the tribe), and he is remembered there as a student who drew and painted constantly.

In 1910 an anthropologist—someone who studies people and their cultures—became interested in Spybuck's art and asked him to paint scenes of the life of the Shawnee and other tribes. At this time the Shawnee lived much like non-Native cattle ranchers and farmers but also kept some of their old ways of life. According to the anthropologist, this painting illustrates the "Chicken Dance," a social dance sometimes called the "Sneak-Up," so named because its movements were like those of the prairie chicken, looking for a mate. The dancers circle around the musicians seated in the center. In this picture of a joyous Shawnee gathering, Spybuck paid close attention to detail, such as different kinds of clothing, and their colors and patterns, and the movements and facial expressions of people.

CORN HUSK DOLL
Clara Red Eye (Seneca, Allegany Reservation, New York). Late nineteenth century.
Corn husk, cloth, glass beads, sequin, yarn (?), and ink. Approximately 8½" h.

16

Would you like to own this doll? Why or why not?

What kinds of games would you play with this doll? How do you think a Seneca child would have played with it?

Describe an ear of corn that you have seen growing or in the grocery store. What do the outer leaves look like? What would they look like if they were dry? Do you think it would be difficult to make a toy out of the dry leaves? How do you think this could be done? If you were going to make a doll or toy figure, how would you do it?

Seneca children played with dolls or toy people in much the same ways as children all over the world do. They pretended that the figures were mothers and fathers, and girls and boys who did chores, played games, and had adventures.

Dolls created by Native American peoples made use of the materials that were available to them. The Seneca, who belonged to a group of peoples called the Iroquois (pronounced "Ir-oh-kwoi"), lived in parts of the northeastern United States where they grew their most important food, corn, along with beans and squash. The corn husk (the dried outer leaves) could be wrapped with string and shaped into a doll or small figure. Some dolls had corn husk bodies and apples for heads.

Corn husk dolls were usually made for Seneca girls by their grandmothers. Grandmothers would make many toys for their grandchildren! The dolls wore colorful clothes that looked just like those of adult men and women. At the time this doll was made, the Seneca dressed much like many of the European people with whom they had come into contact during the 1800s. They wore Native dress only for special occasions. The doll wears a non-traditional flowered coat, yet she also wears leggings and moccasins like the Seneca women of earlier times. This doll has eyes, eyebrows, a nose, and a mouth, but older corn husk figures had no faces. One Seneca story tells of a very lovely doll who was so vain that the Great Spirit took away her beautiful face. The Iroquois peoples also thought that it was up to the children to imagine a face for the doll—happy, sad, or whatever the doll's owner wished.

Point to and name the animals you can find on the side of the canoe. Do these look like animals you have seen? How are they the same? How are they different? Which animals live on land and which live in water?

The artist lived in a place where there were many trees. Is there any way we know this by looking at the canoe?

Find a very small canoe in the picture.

MODEL CANOE
Tomah Joseph (Passamaquoddy). ca. 1905. Birchbark, cedar wood, pitch, iron brads, and basketry splint.
50½" l. × 10½" w. × 8¼" h.

Tomah Joseph (1837–1914) lived on a Passamaquoddy Indian reservation in what we now call Maine. He had several occupations. He was an artist and craftsman but he was also a canoe guide and storyteller. All of these are combined in this model canoe, carved out of the bark, or outer covering, of a birch tree. The designs and illustrations on the sides of the canoe are carved as well. The model was made to be sold to tourists who visited the Maine woods on vacations, however, birchbark art and canoe making already had had a long history among the Eastern Woodlands Indians like the Passamaquoddy.

Living near rivers and surrounded by forests of birch trees, Native peoples of the Northeast traveled on the water in small boats that they made by covering a wooden frame with sheets of birchbark. The bark, which was very strong and stayed dry, but which could be bent and curved, was carefully peeled off the tree without harming it. The parts of

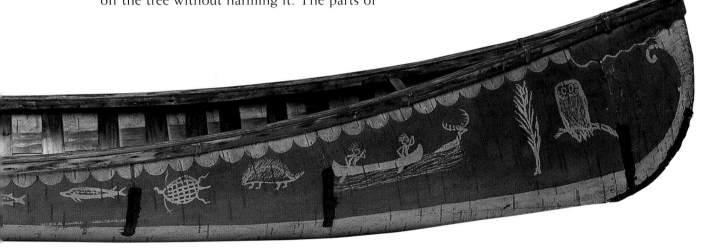

the canoe were tied together with roots, and wooden paddles were used to guide it. A well-made canoe was very lightweight and could be carried on land when traveling on a river became too difficult, or when going from one river to another. It has been said that a birchbark canoe could carry 4,000 pounds! Children played with toy birchbark canoes.

Tomah Joseph's model canoe is decorated with a kind of "picture writing," or story told through pictures, that gives us an idea of what Woodlands people might find on a hunting or fishing trip. The snowy owl, which appears here, was one of Tomah Joseph's favorite characters. The artist often added Passamaquoddy words to his work. On the bow of the model canoe are the words "Kolele Mooke"—good luck.

BOY'S SHIRT
Crow (Montana). Late nineteenth century. Fringed buckskin (?), glass beads, and red wool trade cloth.
33½" l. × 17½" w.

Find and name the different shapes you see on this shirt. Shapes or colors that are repeated make a pattern. Find a pattern on the shirt.

Do you think this shirt was worn every day—for playing? Explain.

How would you feel if you were wearing this shirt?

Do you have a special or favorite piece of clothing? Talk about how it looks.

This very soft leather shirt belonged to a member of the Crow people, one of the Plains Indian groups who lived in what is now Montana, as well as Wyoming and the Dakotas, and who were known for their amazing beadwork. In the 1800s, Native peoples began to receive colored glass beads in trade and started to use them in their decorations. Before they used beads, the Crow and other Plains Indians used porcupine quills, dyed in various colors, to create designs. The Crow would embroider many tiny beads to create geometric shapes and patterns—like diamonds and upside-down triangles, on clothing, moccasins, pouches or bags, and toys. Beading required great patience and skill and the work took a long time. Beadwork and making clothes was mostly, but not only, done by women. Some men also became skilled beadworkers. The fancier the beading, the more important the item, or its owner.

According to the storyteller Joe Medicine Crow, this shirt belonged to a boy rather than to a grown man. This is unusual because it is thought to have been a warrior's shirt. The cut fringes are a type of decoration used by many Plains peoples. Because of the beautiful beading in strips over the shoulders and down the sleeves, it could not have belonged to an ordinary soldier, but perhaps to a chief. It was possible for a boy to be made a chief, but this did not happen very often. Among the Crow, a chief was named by the group and was not always the child of a leader. In the Crow language, the word that comes the closest to "chief" is a word that means "good man." Chiefs, including boy chiefs, were chosen because they lived up to these words.

PETROGLYPH
Sand Tank Canyon, Inyo County, California. Stone (sandstone or basalt). Date unknown.
Figures approximately 8" h.

There are many mysteries in rock art. What kind of animals do you think these are? Do they seem to be all of one kind? Explain your answer.

Does the rock look rough or smooth? Why or why not? Do you think it would be difficult to carve a picture on a rock? How would you do it? How do you think early Native Americans might have done it?

Cover a piece of paper with black or dark-colored pencil and then very carefully erase small sections. You may get an idea of how scraping away a surface creates a design. You can also cover the page with crayon and scratch out parts with a wooden stick or pencil. Try this and describe what you see.

A picture that has been carved or pecked onto the surface of a rock is called a "petroglyph." Thousands of years ago, before the arrival of Europeans, many Native American groups created art by scratching or painting images on the walls of caves or cliffs, or on stones and boulders along travel paths. A picture painted on stone is called a "pictograph." Although we know something about its purpose and how it was made, rock art is still mysterious.

The petroglyph shown here is the oldest object that appears in this book. Although its exact date is not known, it is probably between 1,000 and 1,500 years old. It was found in the mountains of southeastern California. The animals pictured are most likely bighorn or mountain sheep, although some of them could be deer. Mountain sheep were considered the special spirit helpers of shamans (medicine men who talked to the spirit world) who traveled high into the mountains to pray for rain. These rock drawings may have been important in the shamans' work. In the days before written language, petroglyphs also were used to mark the count of a hunt or record the number of days on a journey, or as a kind of message for others from the carver.

Making a petroglyph required a great deal of time. The artist would scrape away at the darker outer layer of rock with a hard, sharpened stone. Gradually, the lighter rock underneath would take the shape of a design or picture.

How do you think this drum would sound? Have you ever played a drum? What did it look like?

When you listen to a drum, can you see anything in your imagination? How do you feel when you listen to rhythms made on a drum?

Describe what you see on the front of the drum (this page). Do the birds seem to be moving fast or slowly? What makes you think so?

Look at the back of the drum (opposite). In what ways did the maker of the drum show that this is a sky at night?

DRUM
Pawnee. ca. 1890. Rawhide, wooden hoop, iron nails and tacks, and pigments.
18" diam. × 3½" deep.

Drums have been used by Native Americans in songs, dances, and rituals for many years. This drum was made by a member of the Pawnee tribe, who had a special use for it.

Until the late 1800s the Pawnee lived on the land that today makes up the states of Nebraska and Kansas. Known as the prairie, this land was mostly flat and had few trees. From the often cloudless prairie, the Pawnee could clearly see the star-filled night sky, and they were famous for their knowledge and drawings of the constellations. Stars occur frequently in Pawnee designs. In 1876 the Pawnee were forced to leave their original lands and move to reservations in Oklahoma. They became increasingly unhappy, as they could no longer live as they had.

Toward the close of the 1800s, a new ceremony called the Ghost Dance spread among the Pawnee. During the ceremony, Ghost Dancers communicated with the spirits of their ancestors and were promised a return to their traditions. The ceremony included the "hand game," an old guessing game that the Pawnee were beginning to forget as they became more like European-Americans in their ways. Two teams played. A player hid a special object in one fist, moving both hands to music to keep the player of the opposite team from guessing which hand was full.

Drums were a central part of the hand-game music. The drumbeat used was very fast, which made the guessing game exciting and difficult. This drum, made from rawhide stretched over a wooden hoop, is said to have been used in the Ghost Dance hand game. It is decorated with images of power, like the Thunderbird, a mighty spirit creature shown swooping down from storm clouds.

WOOD-DUCK EFFIGY BOWL
Middle Mississippian (found near Moundville, Hale County, Alabama). A.D. 1250–1500. Diorite.
Approximately 11¼" l. × 15½" w.

Look at this bowl, made out of stone, and then think about some of the bowls you use. This one is about as large as a medium-sized cooking pot. How heavy do you think it would be if you picked it up? What could it hold? Could you drink with this bowl? Pour with it? Eat with it? Talk about other ways you could use it.

Find and name the different parts of the duck's body. Can you find the duck's wings? The tail?

Does this look like a real duck? Why or why not? What parts look real? Which do not?

How would you decorate something if you couldn't use color? Point to and describe the different kinds of lines on the bowl.

This bowl was made about 600 years ago by ancestors of Native Americans from the southeastern United States. Archaeologists— scientists who study objects and other remains of people who lived in the past—call these early peoples Mound Builders because it was discovered that they had built whole cities on top of great hills, or mounds, of earth. Since the end of the nineteenth century, many of the mounds have been excavated: dug out and the objects underneath removed and brought to museums and places where they are examined. The first Europeans who saw the huge mounds never guessed that they were created by Native peoples, ones who lived many hundreds of years ago.

Looking at ancient objects means looking for clues, like a detective. Archaeologists try to figure out how something was made and for what it was used. This bowl, found buried in a mound in Alabama, was carved from one piece of very hard stone using stone tools. Because of its life-like looks, we can be almost certain that the animal shape of the bowl represents the crested male wood duck. This kind of duck has a long bill and a long neck that allow it to dive under the water. For many ancient Native tribes, water creatures had particular importance.

How many different shapes can you find in these wooden posts carved to look like wolves? How many colors? There are two individual wolf posts—one is shown from the side, the other from the front.

Can you tell that each post was once a single wooden log? What helps you to know this?

These wolves are seven and a half feet tall. What would you think if you saw them? Imagine them looking at you. What would Haida visitors coming to the house in which they were placed think?

If a friend came to your house, how would he or she know that it was your house? What things in it show that this is your house? In what ways is it different from your friend's house? Is it the same in any way?

HOUSE POSTS
Haida. Nineteenth century.
Painted cedar wood.
Each 7½' h.

The identical wolves pictured here are about seven and a half feet tall. These "house posts" probably once stood at either end of the inside back wall of a traditional Haida house as symbols of the clan (a group of related families) that lived there.

The Haida inhabited several groups of small forested islands off the coast of British Columbia in Canada. They enjoyed plentiful natural resources and had traditions in common with the Tlingit and other Native groups that together are known as the Northwest Coast Indians.

The wooden posts were made for a house owner who was wealthy and who would have had the means to afford an expert wood carver, who might need a year or more to complete the job. When the posts were raised, there would be a great feast, the "potlatch." Visitors looking at the house posts would know that the families of the house belonged to the clan symbolized by the wolf. The families had a strong connection to the wolf—and to its qualities, like quickness and strength. The Haida believed people were related to animal spirits and that at times they could change into animals. Natural beings played an important part in Haida mythology. Similar to house posts, totem poles—very tall carvings of many animals and figures, one on top of another, that represented the clan and its history—frequently stood outside at the entrance to a house.

CREST HAT
Tlingit. Nineteenth century. Painted (alder?) wood, spruce root, abalone shell, copper, and hair.
14" h.

Do you wear hats? What kinds? On what occasions?
Does this look like a hat you have ever seen? Explain.

Would you like to wear this hat? Why or why not? How would
you feel wearing this hat?

Do you think the artist tried to make this hat look like a real
bear or an imaginary one? In what ways did the artist make it
look real or make-believe?

How many different colors do you see in this hat? What do
you think it is made of? How big do you think it is? How
heavy? What is your favorite part of the hat?

Crest hats were made for important feasts by long-ago members of the
Tlingit (pronounced "Klink-it") tribe. This group lived on the
southeastern coast of Alaska, near waters that held salmon, sea lions, and
whales, and forests that were home to deer, birds, and bears. All these
natural riches made their way into the work of Tlingit artists, who were
famous for the colorful designs of their clothing and headwear and for
their wood carving.

　　This bear crest hat belonged to a Tlingit clan. A clan is a group of
related families within the Tlingit tribe. It was a treasured possession to
be worn by the various family heads and was thought of as a crown,
symbolizing the spirit of the brown bear. The brown bear, like the one on
the hat, was an important animal to the Tlingit.

　　The hat was usually displayed at "potlatches," feasts celebrating a
birth or a special moment in the life of a family member, or marking a
death. A potlatch included the giving of many valuable gifts and dancing,
music, and storytelling. The number of rings on a crest hat is said to
mean the number of potlatches at which the hat was worn: this hat has
eight rings.

　　The carved wooden bear's twinkling eyes, as well as its ears and
teeth, are made of abalone shell, and its tongue, which is made of copper,
moves. Both copper and abalone shell were considered valuable by the
Tlingit. The "fur" on the bear is human hair.

Look at the pages of this book a second time. Then look at two or three together. In what ways are they different from one another? In what ways are they the same? Choose one for today that you would like to remember.

Look at them all again on another day. Do you notice anything that you didn't see before? On different days, we see things differently, think about them differently.

Keep looking!

PHOTOGRAPH CREDITS